Freedom
of Religion

Freedom of Religion

J. Edward Evans

 Lerner Publications Company · Minneapolis

Front cover photograph by David L. Rose

Cover illustration by George Overlie

Library of Congress Cataloging-in-Publication Data

Evans, J. Edward.
    Freedom of religion / J. Edward Evans.
        p.   cm.
    Includes bibliographical references.
    Summary: Surveys the history of freedom of religion in the
United States and the court cases that defined it.
    ISBN 0-8225-1754-X
    1. Freedom of religion—United States—Juvenile literature.
2. United States—Religion—Juvenile literature. [1. Freedom
of religion.] I. Title.
BR516.E92   1990
323.44′2′0973—dc20   90-34929
                                               CIP
                                               AC

Manufactured in the United States of America

1 2 3 4 5 6 7 8 9 10 99 98 97 96 95 94 93 92 91 90

Contents

Leaders of the Roman Catholic, Jewish, and Protestant faiths gather on the steps of the Tomb of the Unknown Soldier to protest the Vietnam War.

6

1
The Wall of Separation

Religion and politics have long been regarded as two of the subjects most likely to cause arguments in any social gathering. Both involve strong beliefs that are very important to each individual. When an issue involves both religion and politics, as is the case with freedom of religion, it is an open invitation for intense disagreement.

Thomas Jefferson believed that it was best to keep religion and politics as separate as possible. Religion, Jefferson declared, was a matter between God and the individual. Government had no right to interfere with a person's religious opinions. Using a phrase first voiced by 17th-century clergyman Roger Williams, Jefferson wrote in 1802 of the need for a "wall of separation between the Church and State." According to Jefferson, the First Amendment to the United States Constitution set up this wall for the protection of religious freedom. The amendment states, in part, that

> Congress shall make no law respecting an establishment of religion, or prohibiting the free exercise thereof.

In Jefferson's view, the wall of separation was designed to work both ways: to keep the government from interfering with the private beliefs of individuals and the operation of churches, and to keep individuals and churches from imposing their religious beliefs on the rest of the population.

To a large degree, separation has worked to the benefit of both church and state. Half a century after the American Revolution, French historian Alexis de Tocqueville visited the United States and was surprised by the strength and vitality of both its religious and its government institutions. He attributed this healthy state of affairs to the fact that each was independent and free to grow on its own.

The Debate over Religious Freedom

The wall of separation, however, has proven to be a difficult thing to construct and maintain. Government is concerned with establishing and enforcing the rules under which a society operates. Religion is concerned with how a person should live in the service and worship of a higher spiritual authority. Both have

This 19th-century drawing reinforces the principle of separation between church and state. All sects can worship in their own way as long as none of them requires a special privilege in relationship to the state.

8

a great influence on setting the boundaries within which people should live their lives. If both religion and government provide standards for living, how can the two be kept entirely apart? Even James Madison, one of the foremost advocates of church-state separation, admitted the difficulty. Late in his life he observed that it "may not be easy in every possible case to trace the line of separation between the rights of religious and civil authorities."

Most United States citizens believe that some kind of separation is necessary in order to ensure religious freedom for all citizens. It is in deciding exactly where that wall of separation should stand and what it should separate that the debate concerning freedom of religion has grown controversial.

In the United States, the judicial branch of government—the courts—has the responsibility to protect the rights, including the religious rights, of citizens. The courts have the final say in determining which laws are constitutional and which are not. In turn, those decisions determine what freedom of religion means in this country. The courts must make the agonizing decisions over where that wall of separation is to be.

The courts are sworn to base their decisions on the United States Constitution. This document spells out the primary laws by which the country is governed. The Constitution, however, has very little to say about the relationship between religion and government.

The First Amendment is the only constitutional standard that judges have for evaluating cases. This standard is not very precise. The First Amendment does not say what is meant by "establishment of religion." Does it mean only that the government may not set up an official state church? Or does it mean that Congress must stay out of any issue that is even remotely connected to religion? What is "free exercise"? Does it mean that a person is free to break the law while exercising his or her religious beliefs? Even among legal scholars, there is widespread disagreement over the answers to these questions. One of the most striking examples of this can be seen in the opinions of two former Supreme Court justices. Nineteenth-century Justice Joseph Story believed that the "establishment clause" of the First Amendment barred only the creation of an official state church. In 1824, Justice Story said that it was the proper role of government to "foster and encourage the Christian religion generally, as a matter of sound policy as well as revealed truth."

Compare Story's opinion to that of Justice Hugo Black in 1947. Black said that the establishment clause means, among other things, that neither a state nor the federal government can "pass laws which aid one religion, aid all religions, or prefer one religion over another."

Story and Black made their statements when each was sitting on the highest court in the country, the court that has the final say on what freedom of religion means. It is not surprising, then, that there is such debate in the courts as the justices try to apply the words of the First Amendment to the endless variety of cases that come before them. In 1948, Supreme Court Justice Robert Jackson expressed frustration at trying to separate areas of government control from areas of religious freedom. He found nothing in the Constitution or any other legal work to help him make these decisions. "It is a matter in which we can find no law but our own presuppositions," he concluded.

Because of the lack of clear-cut standards, United States citizens are bewildered by what seem to be conflicting laws. Churches are excused from paying property taxes, yet the tuition paid by families to church-sponsored, or **parochial**, schools may not be tax exempt. Public tax money may be used to provide textbooks, but not globes, to parochial schools. The government may hire chaplains to say prayers in the legislature but cannot require a moment of meditation in government-sponsored, or **public**, schools. People who are opposed to all forms of warfare because of their religious beliefs may be excused from military duty, but people whose religious convictions lead them to oppose only a particular war may not.

Our Role in Issues of Religious Freedom

Our history shows that in interpreting the clauses of the Constitution, the government tends to be guided by the wishes of the people. Currently, however, there is a great deal of uncertainty as to what the people of the United States believe. A poll conducted in 1987 found that most U.S. citizens support the separation of church and state as a general principle. Yet the poll found that half of those surveyed believed

Where do we build the wall of separation between church and state?

government should support all religions equally. And when it came to specific issues, such as school prayer, a majority favored government support of religion.

In a democratic republic such as the United States, the opinions of ordinary people can change laws. We can challenge laws that we believe to be unconstitutional, and if the courts agree, the laws are changed. Ideas that are important enough to be included in the Bill of Rights, such as "freedom of religion," are important for us to understand. The best way to understand what "freedom of religion" means and why it is in the Constitution is to study the history of religious freedom. First, this book will outline the events in history that led the writers of the Constitution to guarantee the freedom of religion. Then this book will show how the courts have tried to interpret religious freedom and what the laws now say about this issue.

With this background, we can begin to form our own opinions about the wall of separation between church and state. We can make our own decisions about how we can best preserve our religious freedom and guarantee that the United States is the kind of country we want it to be.

The prosecution of "witches" during the famous witch trials in Salem, Massachusetts, in 1692

2
Legacy of Intolerance

While many religions teach the importance of peace and kindness, history shows that such messages have seldom been taken to heart. Since the beginning of recorded history, people have been killing other people whose religious views differ from theirs. Even though Christians, for example, all believe the Bible to be the word of God, the way in which they interpret the Bible differs. Any deviation from the generally accepted beliefs of the time was **heretical**, and heretics were outlaws. Nearly 2,000 years ago, Romans fed Christians to lions in great open amphitheatres. Holy wars between Christians and Moslems raged 800 years ago. Jews and heretics were brutally slain during the **Inquisitions** that the Roman Catholic church held to find false believers 600 years ago. Most European countries had adopted one religion and forbade the practice of any other. Occasionally, a new king or queen converted to a different religion and outlawed the religion of the previous monarch. When this happened, many previously law-abiding citizens suddenly found themselves to be criminals. In Northern Ireland, Roman Catholics and Protestants have been at war for centuries.

Virginia: Continuing the Tradition

It was from this history of intolerance that the American colonies were founded. The first permanent

In this drawing of religious persecution in the 16th century, Roman Catholics boil, singe, hang, and quarter Protestants.

English settlement was started in 1607 in Jamestown, Virginia. Among the many English customs and attitudes that the settlers brought with them was the European view of religion. It seemed only natural for them to set up an official state church. Since the Virginia founders were loyal English people, that church was the Church of England, or the Anglican church.

Just as in England, all residents of Virginia were taxed to build and support Anglican churches and to support their ministers. Even though other settlers who were not Anglican eventually arrived in Virginia, this did not change. In fact, people who did not agree with the teachings of Virginia's state church were denied the right to build churches of their own.

14

These loyal Anglican colonists enacted severe laws to make sure their established church was the dominant church. In 1614, they passed a law imposing the death penalty for a third offense of breaking, or not resting on, the Sabbath or for speaking disrespectfully about the Christian religion.

At times during the history of the colony, the Anglicans barred Puritans and Quakers from living in Virginia. For a long time, they did not permit Roman Catholics to hold public office, vote, or worship in public. More than 150 years after the colony was founded, members of the established church were still whipping and imprisoning Baptist preachers.

Massachusetts: From Persecuted to Persecutors

In the early 17th century, a group of English Protestants became dissatisfied with the Anglican church. They believed that the church had become too similar to the Roman Catholic church and that its members were not worshipping as God intended. Because they insisted that the church must be "purified," these dissenters became known as Puritans.

As they became more vocal, the Puritans were harassed by the Engglish government. Under King Charles I, the persecution was so bad that a number of Puritans decided to risk crossing the ocean and starting a new life in America. Following another group of Puritans —the Pilgrims—who had come to America in 1620, the new group of Puritans founded a colony in the Massachusetts Bay area in 1630.

Although they were themselves the victims of persecution, they had no intention of helping others obtain religious liberty. The Puritans agreed that there should be one national church. Their only disagreement with the Anglican church had been over policies of the national church. Their goal was to set up a pure Christian society, a "city set upon a hill" to shine the light of Christianity to the world. In fact, the Puritans meant for church and state to be more closely allied than ever.

In such a society, people would live according to the Puritans' interpretation of the Bible. For them, the Bible governed every aspect of life—political views, business activities, and recreation. It dictated what clothing could be worn and how parents should educate their children.

A Pilgrim couple goes to worship.

Attendance at prayer meetings was required. Even an expression of gaiety on a Sunday or a yawn during a sermon carried a penalty. This kind of "ideal" society could exist only if the "right" people belonged to the church and governed the community. Those who wanted to join the official church were thoroughly questioned about their religious experiences and beliefs and about the way they lived. Some were not able to meet the church's rigid standards and were denied membership.

Those who belonged to the established church were so concerned with keeping their community "pure" that they tolerated no disagreement or outside influence on their members. Those who could not live under such rigid restrictions left the established church. In the 1630s, a number of discontented Massachusetts settlers moved to the Connecticut wilderness. Other dissenters were forced out. Anne Hutchinson, a Puritan whose beliefs differed from those accepted by the official church, led prayer meetings at her house with more than 60 people in attendance. She was banished from Massachusetts Bay for disputing the teachings of authorities, and in 1638 she settled in Rhode Island.

Against the wishes of the established church, Anne Hutchinson led prayer meetings in her house in Boston.

When Quakers first arrived in Massachusetts in 1655, they were whipped, imprisoned, and then expelled from the colony. When these measures failed to discourage them from returning to Massachusetts Bay, a law was passed to provide for the hanging of any banished Quaker who returned. Catholic priests were also banned under threat of death. Baptists were, at times, whipped and imprisoned.

A Quakers' meeting in Rhode Island

3
The Idea of Tolerance

Although the degree of intolerance differed from one colony to another, the early colonies followed European tradition. The majority of them either started out with, or eventually established, state churches.

If an individual's beliefs did not conform to those of the state church, he or she was left with little choice. Dissenters were forced to live in the wilderness or to go out and start their own colonies.

Maryland, Rhode Island, and Pennsylvania were all founded by people who were denied freedom to worship elsewhere. It was in these colonies that the ideas, not only of tolerance, but of religious freedom, began to flourish.

Maryland: Roman Catholics and Toleration

In the early 17th century, there was little opportunity for Roman Catholics in England and America to practice their religion openly. It was the dream of an English aristocrat, George Calvert, to establish a haven for Catholics in America. However, he did not live to see his dream fulfilled. Shortly after Calvert died in 1632, the charter of Maryland was granted to his son, Cecil Calvert. He and his brother, Leonard, left England in 1633 and founded the colony of Maryland in 1634.

Maryland was the first colony to guarantee religious freedom to Catholics and Protestants alike. It did so

George Calvert, Lord Baltimore

at least partly out of political necessity. Cecil Calvert knew that in order for his Catholic refuge to survive under the Protestant English government, it must keep the goodwill of Protestants. For this reason, he sought Protestant as well as Catholic settlers for Maryland. In fact, fewer than half of the first arrivals were Catholic. In 1636, Cecil Calvert drew up an oath to be taken by all Maryland governors. The oath promised punishment for anyone who harassed Christians because of their religion.

Trust between religious groups, however, was not so easily formed. In spite of Cecil Calvert's efforts to please Maryland Protestants, they complained to the British government that Catholics dominated the colony. In fear of losing his charter, Calvert appointed a Protestant governor in 1648. This governor, William Stone, invited several hundred Virginia Puritans to move to Maryland to enjoy its religious freedom. Soon they, too, were opposing Calvert's cause.

In an effort to protect Catholics and reassure Protestants who remained suspicious of his intentions, Calvert drafted what became known as Maryland's Act of Toleration. This act, passed in 1649, granted complete freedom of worship to all who believed in Jesus Christ. Protestants in the Maryland Assembly amended the act to eliminate Unitarians from the guarantee. Unitarians believe in the unity of God and reject the doctrine of the Trinity, which says that in God there are three divine beings, the Father, Jesus Christ, and the Holy Spirit.

Maryland's Act of Toleration was not a guarantee of religious freedom. Anyone who did not believe in the Trinity or that Jesus Christ was the son of God was condemned to death. Nevertheless, it did permit different Christian denominations to live as neighbors and worship in their own churches.

Once again, however, Calvert's best intentions were thwarted. In 1649, the Puritans gained control in England and stripped Calvert of his colonial charter. Within five years of its passage, Maryland's Act of Toleration was repealed. Catholics in Maryland were denied the right to vote.

For the next 30 years, the fortunes of Maryland's Catholics rose and fell with the influence of Catholics in the English government. But with the overthrow of the supportive King James II, Catholicism was outlawed in England and the Calvert family's attempt to grant freedom of worship to all Christians in Maryland failed. The Anglican church became the established church of the colony. Catholics again were denied the right to worship in public, and Catholic immigrants were forbidden to come to the colony to live.

Rhode Island: The "Livelie Experiment"

While the Calverts were settling Maryland, a minister named Roger Williams came to Massachusetts Bay Colony from England. Congregational ministers were in short supply in Puritan Massachusetts, so Williams was welcomed upon his arrival in 1631. But in an age when the more deeply religious the person, the more vigorous his or her hatred of other religions, Williams was unique. He declared that people should not be punished for their religious differences.

Williams had other ideas that would influence the future of religious freedom. He disagreed with the Massachusetts system of government, under which public officials handled church business and enforced church rules. What right, he asked, did an impure, earthly government have to judge people in matters of their religious beliefs? Williams believed that the government should stay out of religious concerns. He laid down the principle of separation of church and state 150 years before it was written into the United States Constitution.

Although he preached at some Massachusetts churches, Williams could never accept their connection with the Anglican church. In 1634, he asked his congregation in Salem to renounce the other New England churches and form a church where only true believers worshipped.

Puritan authorities, who had excused some of Williams's earlier outbursts, could tolerate him no longer. He was brought to trial in 1635. The result was a decree by the General Court that:

Whereas, Mr. Roger Williams... hath broached and divulged [diverse] new and dangerous opinions, against the authority of the magistrates; hath also writ letters of defamation, both of the magistrates and churches here... Mr. Williams shall depart out of this jurisdiction... not to return any more without license from the Court.

To avoid being sent back to England, Williams fled from Massachusetts. After wandering in the wilderness for 14 weeks, he purchased land around Narragansett Bay. There he started the settlement of Providence, a community where people of all faiths were welcome. In 1643, he returned to England and obtained a charter for the Providence Plantations, now Rhode Island.

Williams used the English press to spread his new ideas about religious tolerance. He had come to believe that no church could attain the purity he had once sought. Purity

In 1636, Roger Williams bought land around Narragansett Bay from the Native Americans and founded Providence because of "God's providence to him in his distress."

could not be achieved by making everyone in the community believe the same thing. That only led to brutality against those with differing beliefs, a practice that Williams found horrifying. The best thing to do was to let each person pursue his or her own beliefs without government interference.

Many Baptists came to Rhode Island. Of all the sects then in America, they were the most outspoken in their belief in the separation of church and state. Quakers, Jews, and others who had not been allowed to worship freely anywhere in the English-speaking world also found homes in Rhode Island.

Roger Williams eventually severed his ties with organized religion. He called himself a Seeker—he was looking for the truth in religion but did not recognize any one church. He believed that people were entitled to religious freedom as a natural right. Although he personally disagreed strongly with the teachings of the Quakers, he insisted that they have the right to worship, to vote, and to hold public office. Other New England colonies threatened to stop trading with the colony if Rhode Island did not pass anti-Quaker laws. But the people of Rhode Island held fast to their principles.

When changes in the English government required Rhode Island to take out a new charter, the colony's citizens made it clear that they wished to continue their policy of religious freedom. Their wishes were expressed by a Baptist preacher, John Clarke, whose petition to the king stated that the people desired "to be permitted to hold forth, in a livelie experiment that a most flourishing Civill State may stand, yea, and best be maintained...with full libertie of religious concernments."

The new charter was granted in 1663. It went further in its guarantee of religious freedom than any charter ever written when it declared:

> ...that noe person within the sayd colonye, at any tyme hereafter, shall bee any wise molested, punished, disquieted, or called in question, for any difference in opinione in matters of religion which do not actually disturb the civill peace...but that all and everye person...at all tymes hereafter, freelye and fullye have and enjoye his and their own judgments and consciences, in matters of religious concernments...

After the death of Roger Williams in 1683, there was some loss of freedom in Rhode Island. Laws that

Quakers were publicly whipped, and sometimes even killed, for adhering to their religious beliefs.

limited citizenship and eligibility for public office to Protestants were passed. But the influence of Roger Williams, John Clarke, and other early settlers remained with the Rhode Island colonists. These new laws were not strictly observed, and they ceased to be observed at all long before they were repealed. Rhode Island stood as an example to colonists that a civil state could flourish while granting full religious freedom.

Pennsylvania: The Quakers and William Penn

Of all the religious sects in colonial America, none challenged the authority of the established churches and states more than the Society of Friends, commonly called Quakers. Quakers held firm to their beliefs even during periods of extreme persecution. They refused to take the required pledges of loyalty to the government because they did not believe in taking oaths. They refused to remove their hats to anyone in authority because they believed that only God deserved such a gesture of respect. Quakers believed all warfare to be contrary to God's will, and so they refused to carry arms or defend the country.

These beliefs and practices angered people of other religions. Quakers were ridiculed, whipped, banished, and even killed because of their faith. Although the cruel

24

This painting of William Penn's treaty with the Native Americans for Pennsylvania was done by Edward Hicks, an American painter who worked in the primitive style.

treatment was intended to discourage the Quakers' activities, it had the opposite effect. Quakers believed so strongly in their religion that they considered it an honor to suffer for it. Some even went out of their way to preach in the very places where they were most persecuted. A few of those who witnessed such fearlessness in the face of imprisonment and torture could not help but admire the Quakers. One such man was William Penn.

Penn was the son of wealthy and influential parents. Even as a privileged young boy, he had been distressed by injustices suffered by the less fortunate in society. Penn, who had been brought up as a member of the Anglican church, was attracted to Quaker teachings while in his teens. At 23, he made the final break from his family's religion to become a member of the Society of Friends.

William Penn devoted most of his time to giving speeches, participating in debates, and writing letters and pamphlets to promote the Society of Friends. He was thrown into jail several times because of these activities. But, like many other Quakers, he was not discouraged.

In 1677, Penn and other Quakers obtained colonial rights to land in New Jersey. There Penn helped form a plan of government for West Jersey, America's first Quaker colony. Although Quakers believed that their way of life was best, they also believed strongly that everyone had the right to worship according to their own consciences. The West Jersey plan reflected this view:

> No man, nor numbers of men upon earth hath power or authority to rule over men's consciences in religious matters.

The West Jersey plan also set forth ideas that would later be used in the United States Constitution: taxes should not be levied without the consent of the taxed; anyone accused of a crime has the right to a trial by jury.

Because of confusion over legal ownership of land in the Quakers' New Jersey colony, control eventually went to a group of Anglicans. Even so, New Jersey Anglicans continued to tolerate Protestants of all sects.

The West Jersey plan provided Penn with valuable experience, which he used in founding Pennsylvania in 1681. Although the West Jersey plan was partly a business investment, Penn also intended it as a "holy experiment." He wanted to prove that religious freedom, given to responsible citizens, would result in a satisfying life.

Under Pennsylvania's Great Law of 1682, no person acknowledging one God could be penalized in any way because of her or his religion. Nor could anyone be forced to attend any religious service. All faiths could worship and all Christians were guaranteed the right to "serve the government in any capacity, both legislatively and executively."

Pamphlets advertising religious freedom brought settlers from many countries and denominations. Among the sects that settled in Pennsylvania were Catholics, Jews, Lutherans, Mennonites, Quakers, Baptists, Calvinists, and Anglicans. The hostilities and intolerance that had formed over centuries of strict separation were not easily broken down. In Penn's time there was much trouble among the colonists. For a time it seemed impossible for so many denominations to live together peacefully.

Pennsylvania also came under pressure from England to pass laws discriminating against Catholics. Although the colony did give in to some of these demands for a while, Pennsylvania still granted Catholics more religious liberty than any other colony at the time had given them.

As English control over the colonies waned, Pennsylvania granted Catholics full freedom of worship.

Despite the early struggles, Penn's experiment was regarded as a success long before the end of the colonial period. Because the government provided equal protection to all its citizens, most of the disputes between sects were resolved, and Pennsylvanians of widely varying beliefs learned to live together harmoniously.

New York City in the early 1700s: 1 Fort George; 2 Trinity Church; 3 Presbyterian Meeting; 4 North Dutch Church; 5 St. George's Chapel; 6 The Prison; 7 New Brick Meeting; 8 King's College; 9 St. Paul's Church; 10 New Dutch Calvinist Church; 11 Old Dutch Church; 12 Jew's Synagogue; 13 Lutheran Church; 14 The French Church; 15 New Scot's Meeting; 16 Quaker's Meeting; 17 Calvinist Church; 18 Anabaptist Meeting; 19 Moravian Meeting; and 20 New Lutheran Church

A view of New York colonial life down Wall Street past Federal Hall to Trinity Church

4
The Growth of Religious Freedom

At the close of the 17th century, the cause of religious freedom began to make important gains. In 1689, a toleration act was passed in England. The act was in many ways only a grudging concession to religious freedom. It still denied all rights to Catholics and Unitarians in England. It still restricted public office to members of the Anglican church. But it did give most English Protestants the right to worship publicly.

The Toleration Act had only a modest effect on the religious freedom movement in the American colonies. Some colonies ignored the provisions of the act, while others had already progressed far beyond them. There were, however, some basic changes taking place in colonial society that would pave the way for even more freedom.

Increased, Diverse Population

The tradition of a state-supported church caused few problems in England, where whole communities often belonged to a single church. But, with the exception of New England and Virginia, the colonies were populated by more dissenters than members of an established church. As the population grew, the number of dissenting sects in all colonies increased, as did the number of people in those sects. No one religious group was large enough to control all the other groups within a colony.

29

Because of this, a widespread, long-term acceptance of any one religion as the state church would have been impossible.

Economics

For the English government, and for the English people who financed colonial settlements, the colonies were a way to gain wealth. The English did not particularly care who developed the land and built up the trade as long as the work was done. Guarantees of religious freedom were a good means of attracting and keeping hard-working settlers. When persecuted colonial business owners protested to England, they could usually count on powerful English people to act in their behalf.

For example, during the late 17th century, a number of successful Boston business owners were not members of the established church. Their businesses were crucial to the economy of the Massachusetts Bay colony. Yet Massachusetts authorities refused to allow them to vote or to worship in churches of their own. This caused a major split between Massachusetts Puritans, with one group arguing for greater toleration and another group opposing it. In 1686, the Boston business owners appealed to England for help. Aware that these people were making profits for their financiers in England, the English government came to their aid. It revoked the Massachusetts charter. Several years later, a new charter assured these business owners freedom of worship and extended the right to vote to those who were not members of the established church.

Revolution

In the years leading up to the Revolutionary War, colonists became focused on issues of freedom. A series of new taxes levied by the English government on the colonists caused a heated outcry. They protested that they were being denied the rights held by ordinary English people.

By 1775, a majority of the colonists decided that the only way to regain their liberty was to fight for it. During the war that followed, the American colonists won their independence from England. This left the colonies without an established government. They were free to choose whatever form of government they thought was best.

Two ideas had gained influence with some of the leading thinkers of the time. One was the belief that religion is a personal experience—a matter between the individual and God. The other was that people have certain natural rights. Some believed that these rights were given by God. Others believed that they were part of the nature of human beings. Among the most important of these rights was the freedom of all human beings to think for themselves.

Because there was no existing government to resist new ideas, pioneers of American liberty were able to incorporate some of these radical notions into their government. Thomas Jefferson and James Madison, among others, introduced a plan for a free society in which government would exist to serve the people. Ironically, that plan originated in Virginia, a state that had been one of the strongholds of a government-supported church in the American colonies.

George Washington crossing the Delaware River during the Revolutionary War

At the Constitutional Convention, which met in Philadelphia in 1787, delegates drew up a new framework for the government. Two years later, James Madison wrote 10 amendments—the Bill of Rights—that were added to the Constitution.

5

The Constitution
and Religious Freedom

Virginia: The Model

For a long time, Virginia firmly resisted the trend toward religious freedom. The state refused to allow even the minimal rights provided by the 1689 English Toleration Act.

Then in the middle of the 18th century, a Presbyterian minister named Samuel Davies defied officials and traveled to Virginia to preach. Davies sent petition after petition to the Virginia legislature and to England until the state was finally persuaded to adopt the Toleration Act standards. As a result of his work, many Presbyterians moved to Virginia. Their ministers taught and worked for the principle of separation of church and state.

The Presbyterians had a profound influence on some key Virginia legislators, including Patrick Henry. Although he was raised in the Anglican church, Patrick Henry often attended Presbyterian services. The sermons he heard about the meaning of liberty influenced his life. When more than 40 Baptist ministers were whipped, fined, and jailed during a period of persecution from 1768 to 1776, Henry came to their aid. As an attorney, he defended them in court and paid many of their fines himself. When Baptists demanded that they be allowed to preach to their soldiers in the Revolutionary Army, it was Henry who argued and won that right for them.

33

Patrick Henry—"the prophet, the phrase-maker, the orator, the trumpeter of revolt"—speaks to the Virginia Assembly. Standing in the doorway is 22-year-old Thomas Jefferson.

James Madison, an Anglican, studied under John Witherspoon at the College of New Jersey. Witherspoon, a Presbyterian, taught that mere toleration was not enough. The word "toleration" implies that a group that considers itself superior graciously allows inferior groups to worship. Witherspoon urged his students to go beyond religious toleration and to seek religious freedom—the natural right of each person to worship in his or her own way, or not to worship at all. These ideals became Madison's standards. Throughout his many years of service to his country, Madison sought to forever stamp out "the ambitious hope of making laws for the human mind."

Having declared their independence from England in 1776, delegates from the colonies met to draw up a constitution under which their new country would be governed. In Virginia, George Mason was chosen to be the author of the Virginia Constitution and Bill of Rights. The standards of government set forth by Mason provided for more freedom and equality than any government had ever granted. Patrick Henry worked with Mason in writing the sections of the Virginia Bill that stated these principles of religious freedom:

> ...religion or the duty which we owe to our Creator, and the manner of discharging it, can be directed only by reason and conviction, not by force or violence; and, therefore, all men are equally entitled to the free exercise of religion, according to the dictates of conscience; and that it is the mutual duty of all to practice Christian forbearance, love and charity towards each other.

Political leaders such as Thomas Jefferson then attempted to pass laws that would back up such a statement. Of foremost concern was the status of the state church. Both Presbyterians and Lutherans at that time were petitioning for the abolition of the state church. Jefferson also wanted to see the state church abolished. By this time, most Virginians belonged to dissenting sects. Even so, most members of the legislature still belonged to the established Anglican church.

These lawmakers were reluctant to abolish the state church. But they did repeal all laws punishing persons for their religious beliefs and for not attending church services. Dissenters did not have to pay taxes to support the established church.

Thomas Jefferson

In 1779, even Anglicans were permanently excused from the duty of paying taxes to support the church.

Most Virginians had come to accept the idea that government should not levy taxes that would benefit one religion only. But in 1784, they were forced to consider whether it was a threat to religious freedom for government to levy taxes to aid all religion. Patrick Henry believed that religious teaching helped

35

the state preserve the peace by promoting morality and good conduct. For this beneficial service, he believed, religions should receive tax support. Henry proposed a law requiring an annual tax "for the support of the Christian religion, or of some Christian church, denomination or communion of Christians, or for some form of Christian worship."

James Madison saw this as a dangerous abuse of religious freedom. He issued a protest paper, the "Memorial and Remonstrance against Religious Assessments." Among Madison's main points were:

1) Support of religion is a matter of individual conscience. It must be voluntary, not forced.

> ...It is the duty of every man to render the creator such homage, and such only, as he believes to be acceptable to him...

2) Religion does not need to be supported by law.

> ...the establishment proposed by the bill is not requisite for the support of the Christian religion. To say that it is, is a contradiction to the Christian religion itself; for every page of it disavows a dependence on the powers of this world: it is a contradiction to fact; for it is

James Madison

known that this religion both existed and flourished, not only without the support of human laws, but in spite of every opposition from them...

3) Taxation for the support of religion endangers liberty.

> ...the proposed establishment ...distant as it may be, in its present form, from the inquisition, it differs only in degree. The one is the first step, the other the last, in the career of intolerance.

4) Taxation to support religion will make the denominations enemies of one another.

> ...it will destroy the moderation and harmony which the forbearance of our laws to intermeddle with religion has produced among its several sects.

The arguments made by Madison in this paper were so persuasive that they continue to be cited by the courts when debating freedom of religion issues. The immediate effect of protests such as Madison's was to convince the legislature that support of religion was not the government's business. The tax bill was easily defeated in 1785.

The following year the Virginia legislature went further, passing Jefferson's Bill for Establishing Religious Freedom, which had been introduced in 1779, but not voted on until 1786. This guaranteed that:

> ...no man shall be compelled to frequent or support any religious worship, place, or ministry whatsoever, nor shall be enforced, restrained, molested or burdened in his body or goods, nor shall otherwise suffer on account of his religious opinions or beliefs, but...all men shall be free to profess, and by argument to maintain, their opinions in matters of religion, and that the same shall in no way diminish, enlarge, or affect their civil capacities.

With this bill, Virginia became the first state to enact into law full religious freedom. For the first time, religious rights applied not only to various Christian denominations, but also to people of other religions and to **atheists**, or those who believe that God does not exist.

The Constitutional Bill of Rights

During the Revolutionary War, the states sent delegates to a convention to write the Articles of Confederation. These articles were meant to define federal government issues separate from the states' constitutions. By 1786, it became clear that a group of states could not function as a nation and needed a stronger foundation. The states again sent delegates to a convention. The delegates decided not to revise the Articles of Confederation, but to write a new Constitution. This Constitution was drawn up to define the powers and duties of the national government of the United States.

The only mention of religion in the entire document was the statement that "...no religious Test shall ever be required as a Qualification to any Office or public Trust under the United States." Most of the framers of the Constitution agreed that they needed to say no more on the subject. Since religion was nowhere else mentioned in the Constitution, the federal government had no power to act upon matters of religion.

Politicians such as George Mason and Patrick Henry, however, were skeptical. The evidence of history and of their own experience convinced them that one should never assume that governments will act in a particular way. Many of the states ratified the Constitution only after they were assured that the first Congress would amend it to spell out specific rights with which the government could not interfere.

Working from the principles set out during the early Virginia debates, James Madison drafted the amendments desired by the states. Of the 12 recommended amendments, 10 were ratified in 1791. They became known as the Bill of Rights.

Patrick Henry speaking in the first Continental Congress

To guarantee religious freedom, the wording "Congress shall make no law respecting an establishment of religion, or prohibiting the free exercise thereof..." was purposely crafted as a double protection. Madison believed that the establishment of government support for religion must be prohibited in order for religious freedom to be safe.

States' Restrictions on Religious Liberty

The passage of the First Amendment did not guarantee full religious freedom in the United States. It only meant that the federal government could not infringe upon these liberties. The state governments were still free to impose restrictions on religious freedom.

Many of the states did retain some of their former restrictions. Some insisted that holders of public office had to be Christians. Other states required public officials to take an oath saying that they believed in God. Some states continued to tax citizens for the support of religious institutions. Some states continued to deny voting rights to Catholics and to non-Christians.

Although the Bill of Rights did not have the authority to override these restrictions on religious rights, it did succeed in promoting the idea of religious freedom. Citizens of the states began to insist that the old laws be repealed. Some states acted quickly to guarantee full freedom of worship, and separation of church and state. Others acted more slowly. Massachusetts did not abolish its established churches until 1833. In 1877, New Hampshire still required public officials to swear to their belief in Christianity.

Eventually, every state prohibited taxation for the support of religious institutions and dropped its religious requirement for voting. In every state, toleration evolved into freedom. Instead of merely *allowing* people of all faiths to worship, Americans recognized the *right* of people of all faiths to worship. A wall of separation between church and state was firmly in place.

The 14th Amendment and Religious Freedom

In 1925, the task of defining and maintaining that wall shifted from the states to the federal government. That year, the United States Supreme Court ruled that the guarantees of liberty in the Constitution also applied to the states. The Court used

These members of the 1925 Supreme Court were the first to rule that individual states could not restrict the rights guaranteed by the Constitution. Soon after their ruling, the Court began to hear more cases in which people claimed their constitutional rights had been violated.

the 14th Amendment, adopted in 1868, as the basis for granting this greater protection. The 14th Amendment forbids states to deprive citizens of equal protection of the law, or to deprive them of life, liberty, or property without due process of law.

This decision marked the beginning of a new era in the history of religious liberty, for it meant that individuals who believed that the actions of any branch of government interfered with liberty of conscience could appeal their case to the nation's highest court.

The Supreme Court

The Supreme Court is made up of nine members—one chief justice and eight associate justices. The majority of the cases it considers are requests to review decisions that have been made by state or lower federal courts. The Supreme Court can refuse to hear these appeals. It accepts only those cases that raise important issues of federal constitutional law.

After hearing arguments and studying written statements from lawyers representing each side of an

Justices on the 1990 Supreme Court are, seated, left to right, *Thurgood Marshall, William Brennan, Chief Justice William Rehnquist, Byron White, Harry Blackmun,* standing *Antonin Scalia, John Paul Stevens, Sandra Day O'Connor, and Anthony Kennedy.*

issue, the justices vote to determine a ruling. One of the justices prepares a statement called the opinion of the Court, giving the reasons for the ruling. When the justices do not agree, both a majority and a minority, or dissenting, opinion may be prepared. In addition, any justice wishing to add his or her own views to those expressed in the majority or minority opinion may write a separate statement.

As American ideas about liberty and equality change, new Supreme Court decisions reflect those changes. Yet at the same time, the Court has shown that it is ready to uphold the principles of the Constitution even when the majority of Americans oppose them. In reaching its decisions, the Supreme Court must first interpret the Constitution and then apply it to modern times. As the following chapters reveal, this has been a difficult and delicate task, and Supreme Court decisions have profoundly affected life in the United States.

Some of the people who believe that religious training is an important part of education send their children to parochial schools, such as this elementary school. They also pay taxes, which support public schools.

6
Government Aid to Religion in the Schools

"Congress shall make no law respecting an establishment of religion..."

The establishment clause, cited above, raises the question of government aid to religion. Government can aid religion in two ways. The first is through the passage of laws or regulations that help one or several religions to spread their doctrines. A requirement that public schools start their day with a prayer would be in this category. The second aid government can offer to religion is funds to benefit one or all religious institutions. A government grant of funds to build a Sunday school building would be an example of this type of aid.

The main place where establishment-clause issues have been fought is the classroom. The United States government wants to provide an education for all children. Many people believe that religious training is an important part of education. How, then, can government provide support for education without supporting religion?

State Aid to Parochial Schools

The first important Supreme Court decision regarding the establishment clause was made in 1947. According to New Jersey law, local school boards could reimburse parents for money they spent to send their children to and from school on public buses. Even parents whose children attended parochial schools could be reimbursed. In the case of *Everson v. Board of Education*, the Supreme Court was asked to decide if tax money to pay for transportation to parochial schools violated the First Amendment.

To make their decision, the justices on the Court studied the meaning and purpose of the establishment clause. Basing his understanding on the writings of Jefferson and Madison, Justice Hugo Black said that the establishment clause means this:

♦ Neither a state nor the federal government can set up a church.

♦ Neither can pass laws which aid one religion, aid all religions, or prefer one religion over another.

♦ Neither can force or influence people to go to or to remain away from church against their will or force them to profess a belief or disbelief in any religion.

♦ No one can be punished for entertaining or professing religious beliefs or disbeliefs, for church attendance or non-attendance.

♦ No tax can be levied to support any religious activities or institutions.

♦ Neither a state nor the federal government can, openly or secretly,

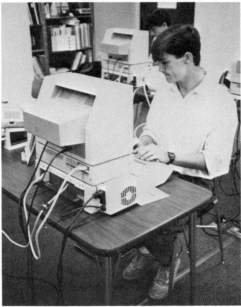

Because the state has a responsibility to educate people, but not to aid religion, there is a question of whether state taxes should pay for the books and computers these students use at parochial schools.

participate in the affairs of any religious organizations or groups and vice versa.

Using these criteria, Black and four other justices decided that the New Jersey law did not violate the Constitution. Black wrote the opinion for the majority, and in it he said that the law "does no more than provide a general program to help parents get their children, regardless of their religion, safely and expeditiously to and from accredited schools."

Four other justices, although they agreed with Black's list of limitations, thought the law was unconstitutional. Writing for the minority, Justice Wiley Rutledge said,

> Does New Jersey's action furnish support for religion by use of the taxing power? Certainly it does...Here parents pay money to send their children to parochial schools and funds raised by taxation are used to reimburse them. It aids them in a substantial way to get the very thing which they are sent to the particular school to secure, namely religious training and teaching.

Rutledge's opinion suggested that if a law allowing government to finance transportation to religious schools was considered public welfare legislation in support of

45

education, then "there could be no possible objection to more extensive support of religious education by New Jersey."

After the *Everson* case, the Supreme Court did not rule on the issue of government aid to children in religious schools again until 1968, when the textbook loan case came before the Court. The case was brought to the Court by two boards of education in New York. It involved a New York state law that required public school boards to supply textbooks, without charge, to all children in the school district who were enrolled in grades 7 through 12 of a public or private school. Parochial school children were included. The books were the property of the public boards of education and were loaned to the children, who used them for their class work but did not keep them. Parochial school authorities could choose which books they wanted to use, but each choice had to be approved by the public school authorities, and only nonreligious books could be provided by this program.

The Supreme Court ruled, in a 6-3 vote, that the New York law did not violate the Constitution. Justice Byron White, in writing the majority opinion, said that the key

Supreme Court Justice Hugo Black

issue was whether or not the main purpose or effect of the law was to aid or harm religion. If so, it was unconstitutional. If not, the law was valid even if it happened to aid religion.

The Court concluded that the New York law was aimed at making educational opportunities available to students. In the opinion of the majority, the books were not furnished to the schools but to the students, for the benefit of parents and children.

Justice Black cast a dissenting opinion. He called the New York

Supreme Court Justice William Brennan

law a "flat, flagrant, open violation of the First and Fourteenth Amendments." In comparing this case to the Everson case, Black declared that there was a great difference between "books, which are the heart of any school," and "bus fares, which provide a convenient and helpful general public transportation service."

The two decisions did not provide clear guidelines for what a government could or could not do to aid education. A third case arose a few years later. At issue in the case of *Lemon v. Kurtzman* was a Rhode Island plan for the state to provide a 5 percent salary supplement for teachers in private schools.

Justice William Brennan used past decisions to devise a specific three-part test of the establishment clause:

1) A law must have a secular [nonreligious] purpose.

2) The principal effect of the law must neither advance nor inhibit the cause of religion.

3) The law must not foster excessive entanglement with religion. According to Brennan, a law could be considered constitutional only if it passed all three parts of the test. In the *Lemon* case, the Rhode Island law failed to pass the test and was declared unconstitutional. Brennan's three-part test has since been relied on as a guide to making decisions not only in school aid cases but in most matters concerning the establishment clause.

Religious Instruction during Public School Hours

In 1948, the Supreme Court faced the issue of whether students could be allowed to take religious classes in public school classrooms during school hours. Religious classes were offered once a week in schools in Champaign, Illinois, for students who had parental permission to participate. Students who did not attend were sent to other rooms where they did their class work. There was no cost to the state because the religious instructors were paid by a voluntary interfaith group, the Champaign Council on Religious Education. Instructors did need to be approved, however, by the superintendent of schools.

Vashti McCollum, the mother of a Champaign student, brought suit to prohibit the religious instruction program. In the case of *McCollum v. Board of Education*, the Supreme Court reached a near-unanimous decision. With only one dissenter, the Court found that the program did violate the establishment clause.

Justice Black delivered the majority opinion:

> Pupils compelled by law to go to school for secular education are released in part from their legal duty upon the condition that they attend the religious classes. This is beyond all question a utilization of the tax-established and tax-supported public school system to aid religious groups to spread their faith.

This decision led to another question. Would such a program of religious instruction be legal if it were offered outside of the public school? The 1952 case of *Zorach v. Clauson* concerned such a program offered in New York. Again, students were released from class upon written request from their parents. Those who were not released stayed in the classrooms. Attendance reports were sent to the schools to verify that the released children had reported for religious instruction.

In a 6-3 vote, the Court approved the New York program. Justice William Douglas stated:

Should public school students be allowed to participate in religious instruction during school hours?

We are a religious people whose institutions presuppose a Supreme Being...When the state encourages religious instruction or cooperates with religious authorities by adjusting the schedule of public events to sectarian needs, it follows the best of our traditions...To hold that it may not would be to find in the Constitution a requirement that the government show a callous indifference to religious groups. That would be preferring those who believe in no religion over those who do believe.

Justice Robert Jackson disagreed and offered this counterargument:

If public education were taking so much of the pupils' time as to injure the public or the students' welfare by encroaching upon their religious opportunity, simply shortening everyone's school day would facilitate voluntary and optional attendance at church classes...As one whose children, as a matter of free choice, have been sent to privately supported church schools, I may challenge the Court's suggestion that opposition to this plan can only be anti religious, atheistic, or agnostic. My evangelistic brethren confuse an objection to compulsion with an objection to religion.

Prayer and Bible Reading in Public Schools

According to a variety of polls, more than two-thirds of the voters in the United States favor scheduling a time for prayer in the public schools. Thus, Supreme Court rulings outlawing this practice have repeatedly drawn a hostile response from the public.

The Court's decision on the 1962 case of *Engel v. Vitale*, often referred to as the Regents' Prayer Case, drew a particularly hostile response. The New York Board of Regents, which governs the state's public schools, composed this prayer: "Almighty God, we acknowledge our dependence upon Thee, and we beg Thy blessings upon us, our parents, our teachers, and our country." The regents recommended that the prayer be recited each morning in New York public schools.

While not all of New York's local school boards acted upon the regents' recommendation, the New Hyde Park Board of Education did. In response, the parents of 10 pupils challenged the legality of the use of this prayer in public schools. The board of education defended the use of the regents' prayer by saying it was nondenominational and that no one was forced to recite it. Children who objected to saying the prayer were allowed to remain silent or could, if they wished, leave the room.

The Supreme Court sided with the parents. Justice Black delivered the opinion. Noting "the historical fact that governmentally established religions and religious persecutions go hand in hand," Black said that the authors of the First Amendment wrote the ban on establishment of religion:

> ...to quiet well-justified fears which nearly all of them felt arising out of an awareness that governments of the past had shackled men's tongues to make them speak only the religious thoughts that government wanted them to speak and to pray only to the God that government wanted them to pray to. It is neither sacrilegious nor anti religious to say that each separate government in this country should stay out of the business of writing or sanctioning official prayers and leave that purely religious function to the people themselves and in those the people choose to look to for religious guidance.

Regarding the claim that participation was voluntary, Black replied that the ban on the enactment of

Many cases have come before the Supreme Court questioning the constitutionality of Bible reading in the public schools.

laws that establish an official religion "is violated by the enactment of laws which establish an official religion whether those laws operate directly to coerce nonobserving individuals or not."

Only one justice, Potter Stewart, disagreed with the verdict. Stewart wrote that he did not see how an official religion was "established by letting those who want to say a prayer say it." In fact, he believed that removal of prayer from public schools amounted to an establishment of the "religion" of **secularism**, or the rejection of religion.

The majority of the public sided with Stewart, and reacted with anger to the decision. One member of Congress called it the most tragic decision in the history of the United States; another said it was a blow to all believers in a Supreme Being. Ninety-six members of Congress published an attack on the Court. The uproar impelled President John Kennedy to issue a statement on the matter. Kennedy noted that prayer at home and in churches would give children a much more meaningful concept of prayer than the recitation of prayers in school.

Giving their children a more meaningful concept of prayer, according to President Kennedy, this family asks a blessing at home.

Some religious leaders added that nondenominational prayers—which, by nature, were so bland and vague as to be almost meaningless—were hardly good examples of the function of prayer.

The controversy over the decision had scarcely died down before two similar cases came before the Court. One involved a Pennsylvania law requiring that each public school day begin with the reading, without comment, of 10 verses from the Bible. Any child could be excused from participating in the Bible reading or could leave the room upon written request from their parents.

At Abington Senior High School, the Bible passages were read by selected students and were broadcast into each homeroom through an intercom system. Following this, students in the classrooms were asked to stand and join in a recitation of the Lord's Prayer.

Edward Schempp, whose children attended the Abington school, brought suit in 1963 to determine the constitutionality of the law. Schempp testified that the Bible passages presented doctrines that were contrary to the teachings of his family's Unitarian faith. He did not want his children excused from the room because he felt that this would affect their relationship with their teachers and other students.

At the same time, opening exercises in the Baltimore public schools consisted of a Bible reading or a recitation of the Lord's Prayer. Madalyn Murray, and her son William J. Murray III, a student in a Baltimore public school, were professed atheists. The Murrays filed suit to have the Baltimore religious exercises declared unconstitutional.

The Supreme Court made one ruling that applied to both the Abington and the Baltimore cases. It found that religious exercises, when conducted as part of the regular activities of public school students, violated the establishment clause.

Justice Thomas Clark, writing for the majority, argued that the Court was not denying people the right to exercise their religion. It was merely preventing them from using the "machinery of the State to practice [their] beliefs." Clark responded to the renewed argument that the encroachment on religious freedom was minor. Echoing the words of Madison and Black, he wrote, "The breach of neutrality [by governments] that is today a trickling stream may all too soon become a raging torrent."

Following the Supreme Court rulings in the prayer and Bible reading cases, more than 100 members of Congress introduced measures to amend the Constitution. These measures would have reworded the First Amendment to permit Bible reading and recitation of prayers in public schools.

During 1963 and 1964, Congress held public hearings on the proposed changes. As the proposals were discussed and debated, however, it became clear that there was no way to reword the amendment without a resulting loss of liberty. The First Amendment remained unchanged.

The school prayer issue, however, was not resolved. In DeKalb County, Illinois, kindergarten children recited the following prayer before they had their morning snack:

> We thank you for the flowers so sweet,
> We thank you for the food we eat,
> We thank you for the birds that sing,
> We thank you for everything.

The parents of one of the kindergarten children sued on the grounds that the Supreme Court had banned prayer in public schools.

The lower courts noted that, although the verse was hardly imposing a religious doctrine, it was a prayer. In 1968, the Supreme Court ruled that because it was a prayer, it could not be recited as part of a public school's daily activities.

For a time, there was relatively little opposition to the Court's ban on school prayer. With the acceptance of Brennan's three-part test for violations of the establishment clause, it was clear that school prayer could not survive in the courts. Some schools continued to hold religious exercises in violation of the Supreme Court ruling. As long as parents of the children attending the school did not protest, such practices could continue.

Active support for school prayer revived in the late 1970s. In 1978, the Alabama legislature passed a law allowing teachers of grades one through six to announce a one-minute period of silence for meditation at the start of each day. Three years later it went further, allowing teachers to announce that a period of silence "not to exceed one minute in duration shall be observed for meditation and voluntary prayer." In 1982, Alabama added that any teacher could lead willing students in a state-composed prayer. Meanwhile, the Republican party platform in 1980 called on government to "restore the right of individuals to participate in voluntary, nondenominational prayer in public schools."

In 1985, however, the Supreme Court reaffirmed that the Constitution prohibited government

In 1968, the Supreme Court decided that it was unconstitutional for preschoolers to be led in prayer before their snack.

from organizing religious activities of any kind. In a 6-3 vote, the Court declared that even Alabama's scheduled daily moment of silence for "meditation or voluntary prayer" went beyond the limits of the law. The Court made it clear that it was not opposed to prayer in schools and that students were free to offer silent prayers whenever they chose. Its objection was to the state's involvement.

In the Court's opinion, the Alabama law was designed simply to bypass the 1962 ruling outlawing state-mandated prayer in public schools. Since its purpose was religious, the law was unconstitutional.

Evolution v. Creationism in the Public Schools

In 1858, Charles Darwin presented his theory of **evolution** by the "survival of the fittest." He proposed that modern species of living things evolved from more primitive forms of life that first appeared on Earth millions of years ago. A bitter controversy among scientists, religious leaders, and the general public arose. But Darwin's theory of evolution became accepted by biologists as a sound explanation of how living things, through many generations, had changed and adapted to their environment.

Some Christians believed that the theory of evolution contradicted the **creation** story found in the Book of Genesis, part of the Bible. The idea that an "anti-religious doctrine" was being taught to their children in public schools enraged them. In 1925, the state of Tennessee passed a law making it illegal for any publicly funded school in the state to "teach any theory that denies the story of the Divine creation of man as taught in the Bible, and to teach instead that man has descended from a lower order of animals."

John Scopes, a biology teacher at Central High School in Dayton, Tennessee, decided to test the law. He used a book called *A Civic Biology* by George William Hunter to teach the theory of evolution in his classroom. Scopes was arrested.

The resulting "Monkey Trial," so named because of Darwin's theory that humans and apes evolved from the same ancestor, ignited strong feelings across the nation. Former presidential candidate William Jennings Bryan joined the prosecution, and the respected trial lawyer Clarence Darrow argued on behalf of Scopes. Scopes was found guilty of breaking the law and was fined.

The court's decision led to statutes banning the teaching of evolution in other states. These lasted until 1968 when the Supreme Court took up the case of *Epperson v. Arkansas*. In a unanimous decision, the Court reversed the rulings of the Scopes trial. The theory of evolution had been singled out for censorship solely because it was said to conflict with a religious doctrine. The Arkansas law banning the teaching

In the 1960 movie, Inherit the Wind, *the Scopes "Monkey Trial" and the events surrounding it were reinacted.*

of evolution could claim no other purpose than to bolster this religious doctrine. Therefore it was declared unconstitutional.

Creationists then took a new approach. Since they could not legally ban the teaching of evolution, they instead insisted that the theory of creationism be presented by the schools as an alternative to evolution. The state of Arkansas agreed and passed legislation—the 1981 Arkansas Act 590—requiring that biology teachers give "equal time" to the presentation of the biblical theory of creation.

The scientific community was outraged. They protested that scientific evidence overwhelmingly supported the theory of evolution. They claimed, and were backed by a number of religious scholars, that creationists were confusing the fields of science and religion. Evolution, as a science, was not concerned with life's ultimate origins. It only explained how nature appeared to operate. The Book of Genesis, on the other hand, was a religious work, concerned with life's ultimate origins, not with scientific analysis.

The matter was taken to the courts. In January of 1982, in the case of *McLean v. Arkansas*, U.S. District Judge William R. Overton ruled that the Arkansas law violated the First Amendment. According to Judge Overton,

The trial scene from the movie **Inherit the Wind.**

The only inference which can be drawn from these circumstances is that the Act was passed with the specific purpose by the General Assembly of advancing religion.... No group, no matter how large or small, may use the organs of government, of which the public schools are the most conspicuous and influential, to foist its religious beliefs on others.... An injunction will be entered permanently prohibiting enforcement of Act 590.

This ruling prompted another judge to strike down, without trial, a similar law passed in Louisiana in 1981. It was this case, *Edwards v. Aguillard*, that made its way to the Supreme Court in 1987.

Those in favor of the Louisiana law argued that creationism was not just a religious doctrine but a science. They presented their own evidence indicating that all forms of life now on Earth first appeared only a few thousand years ago. The purpose of the law, they said, was merely to give their children a balanced education.

But by a vote of 7 to 2, the Supreme Court rejected the claims of the creationists. Writing for the majority, William Brennan pointed out that any biology teacher who wanted to teach creationism was free to do so. The problem with the Louisiana law was that it discriminated in favor of creationism. It sought to "employ the symbolic and financial support of government to achieve a religious purpose." According to the Court, this was exactly what the First Amendment was designed to prevent.

57

This Nativity scene was part of the "Christmas Pageant for Peace" near the White House in Washington, D.C.

7
Establishment Issues outside School

Although school-related issues have dominated the discussion in modern times, schools are not the only arenas of conflict regarding the establishment clause. The courts have had to decide whether or not government was supporting religion in other areas as well.

Sunday Closing

Many states have enacted laws prohibiting various kinds of business transactions from taking place on Sunday. In 1961, the Supreme Court was asked to decide whether or not these laws were constitutional.

The case presented to the Court involved Margaret McGowan and her fellow employees at a discount department store in Maryland. They were convicted of selling such items as floor wax and staples in violation of a state law that restricted Sunday sales to "essential" items.

Critics of the law charged that the purpose of this government-mandated closing was to advance the cause of a particular religion. It was meant to reinforce the Christian **Sabbath**, or day of rest, which Christians traditionally observe on Sunday. They believed that the state was establishing this doctrine of the majority as law.

The Supreme Court, however, upheld the Sunday closing laws. It conceded that such a tradition had its roots in religion. But according to Chief Justice Earl Warren, Sunday closing had begun to take on a secular nature sometime in the 18th century. Currently, he concluded, it served a secular purpose. The primary effect of the law was to promote relaxation, not religion. States were well within their rights to pass laws in the interests of public health, safety, and welfare.

That same year the Court rejected a protest from an Orthodox Jew who was forced by law to close on Sunday even though his own religion required him to close on Saturday as well.

Religious Requirement for Public Office

Even before the Bill of Rights was adopted, the Constitution stated that no religious test would ever be required as a qualification for public office. In the 1920s, the Supreme Court ruled that constitutional guarantees of freedom must be observed by states as well as by the federal government. Yet eight states continued to require all public officials to take an oath declaring their belief in God.

This requirement was finally challenged in the case of *Torcaso v. Watkins* in 1961. Roy Torcaso had been denied a commission as **notary public**, an official witness, by the state of Maryland because he refused to swear that he believed in God. Torcaso's suit was unanimously upheld by the Supreme Court. That decision automatically struck down the requirements for a religious oath of office in the seven other states.

Taxation of Church Property and Income

The United States Internal Revenue Service does not tax churches, church schools, or religious groups for the income they receive as charities. State laws provide similar **exemptions**, an amount of money not subject to taxation, for religious groups. Individuals can also deduct the amounts they give to religious associations from their taxes.

Some people have argued that by excusing churches from paying taxes, the government gives them special treatment. In this way, the government is said to be aiding the establishment of religion.

On the other side, people argue that the government's power to tax gives it the power to control. Religious institutions are specifically held by the Constitution to be outside the control of government. In

The Minnesota Orchestra, a nonprofit organization, which, like a church, is tax exempt.

addition, nonprofit educational or service organizations—National Public Radio, the American Heart Association, the American Ballet Theatre—are not taxed. Religious organizations are considered part of this group in view of the education they provide and the public services they perform.

The issue of churches and taxes came before the Supreme Court in the 1970 case of *Walz v. Tax Commission.* In an 8-1 decision, the Court upheld the right of the government to allow such exemptions. Chief Justice Warren Burger wrote that this was a situation in which the government could help religion. "Either course," he wrote, "taxation of churches or exemption, occasions some degree of involvement with religion." The purpose of the First Amendment was to avoid government involvement with religion as much as possible. Burger pointed out that tax exemption limited rather than enlarged the area of government entanglement and this was closer to the design of the Constitution.

Public Displays of Nativity Scenes

A similar secular basis was found by the Court for the public funding of a **Nativity** scene—a scene depicting the birth of Jesus. In 1984, authorities in Pawtucket, Rhode

A Nativity scene outside city hall in Pawtucket, Rhode Island

the accommodation of religion. More importantly, according to the majority, Christmas has become a national secular holiday, despite its religious origin. Therefore the Nativity scene filled "essentially a secular purpose."

This controversial decision illustrates the complexities of freedom of religion cases. Many who favored more religious influence in society applauded the result. But although the decision weakened the wall of separation between church and state, it also had the effect of reducing one of Christianity's most sacred symbols, the Nativity scene, to an official classification as a nonreligious symbol.

Chaplains

According to the courts, no branch of government can use funds collected from the general public to pay for any wholly religious purpose. Yet the government has employed and paid chaplains in both the armed forces and legislatures since the founding of the United States.

The employment of chaplains is clearly a government establishment of religion. Yet it has been judged necessary for several reasons. One of these is that chaplains are needed

Island, approved the public funding of a Nativity scene in a park by a public shopping center. Opponents of the funding claimed that this was a blatant use of government power to promote a particular religion, and they filed suit.

Lower courts ruled that the public funding was indeed unconstitutional. But by a 5-4 vote, the Court upheld the right of the city to act as it did. The majority agreed that the Constitution firmly mandated

A chaplain leading a prayer in the Minnesota House of Representatives

in order to comply with the "free exercise" clause of the First Amendment. Armed forces chaplains must be provided in order to allow soldiers the free exercise of their religious beliefs.

A Supreme Court case involving chaplains occurred in 1983 in the case of *Marsh v. Chambers*. In a 6-3 decision, the Court ruled that the state of Nebraska could pay a chaplain to conduct prayers at the start of legislative sessions. The basis for this decision was that chaplains were used in such functions by the very people who wrote the First Amendment. Chief Justice Burger reasoned that because legislative chaplains were provided for at the First Continental Congress, the framers of the establishment clause clearly did not consider that practice a threat to the separation of church and state.

63

This drawing depicts a Native American peyote ceremony. In 1990, the Supreme Court upheld the dismissal of two Native Americans from their jobs because they had used peyote in a religious ceremony. The Court stated that when religious rights clash with the government's need for uniform rules, the Court would side with the government.

8
The Free Exercise of Religion

"... Or prohibiting the free exercise thereof."

In his "wall of separation" letter, Thomas Jefferson wrote that "the legislative powers of government reach actions only, and not opinions." But many people are influenced by their religious opinions to act in a certain way. So when the First Amendment guarantees that Congress cannot pass laws prohibiting the free exercise of religion, what does it mean? Does it protect only opinions? Or does free exercise give the individual the right to break the law when those laws conflict with his or her religious beliefs? These questions are at the heart of court cases involving the free exercise clause of the First Amendment.

The first important free exercise case came to the attention of the Supreme Court in 1879. At that time the Church of Jesus Christ of Latter-day Saints—also known as the Mormon church—taught that Mormon men should practice **polygyny**, which means for a man to be married to more than one woman at the same time. George Reynolds, a Mormon living in the Utah territory, felt he had no choice but to follow this practice or be punished by "damnation in the life to come."

But polygyny was a violation of United States law. The Supreme Court was called on to decide if the polygyny law infringed upon Reynolds's constitutional right to freely exercise his religion.

In the 1840s, Mormon pioneers crossed the Great Plains above *and established the Utah territory. These Mormans were imprisoned for practicing polygyny* left.

The Court decided that it did not. In upholding Reynolds's conviction, the Court said: "Laws are made for the government of actions, and while they cannot interfere with mere religious belief and opinions, they may with practices." If the government were not allowed to place any restrictions on what people could do in the name of their religion, this would "permit every citizen to become a law unto himself. Government could exist only in name under such circumstances."

The Court reaffirmed its decision in a 1990 case, which involved two Native American men who ingested peyote—a drug—as a traditional sacrament of Native American religions. The use of peyote is banned by law and the men were fired from their jobs and denied unemployment benefits. In a 6-3 vote, the Supreme Court upheld their dismissal, stating that it would no longer shield believers whose religious practices violate general laws. Writing for the majority, Justice Antonin Scalia declared that when religious rights clash with the government's need for uniform rules, the Court would side with the government.

Although she voted with the majority, Justice Sandra Day O'Connor stated that Scalia's opinion "is incompatible with our nation's fundamental commitment to individual religious liberty."

Sanctuary

Generally, the courts have affirmed the Reynolds decision. People who take actions that violate the law are held accountable, regardless of the religious convictions that led to the action. Examples of this principle have been found in cases involving the sanctuary movement.

For centuries, government authorities have refrained from making arrests in sacred places, such as churches. Churches have used this tradition to provide **sanctuary**, or protection, for those whom church members see as being treated unjustly by the government. During the early 1980s, hundreds of United States churches, more than a dozen cities, and the state of New Mexico provided sanctuary for refugees fleeing from oppression in Central America. These refugees were considered illegal aliens by the United States government, and sheltering them was a federal crime.

Eventually one of the most active sanctuary churches, Southside United Presbyterian Church in Tucson, Arizona, was targeted for prosecution by the government. Government informants infiltrated Bible studies and congregational meetings. Based on evidence gathered by these informants, the church's pastor, Reverend John Fife, and several others were brought to trial. Although Fife's actions were based on his religious convictions, the judge in the case declared that he would not allow any defense based on religious beliefs. In 1986, Fife and five other church workers were convicted of criminal conspiracy and 12 other counts. Some of the churches involved have since filed suit against the government claiming that the government spying within a church violated the First Amendment free exercise clause.

"Obnoxious" Religion and Disturbance of the Peace

There have been some cases in which convictions have been reversed because the laws on which they were based were later found to be too restrictive of an individual's right to practice religion. In 1940, three Jehovah's Witnesses—Newton Cantwell and his sons, Jesse and Russell—attempted to spread their faith to others. They set up a phonograph on a public street in a predominantly Roman Catholic neighborhood in Connecticut to broadcast their views. Included in their activities were attacks on the Roman Catholic faith and door-to-door selling of religious materials. The Cantwells were arrested and convicted both of inciting a breach of the peace and of soliciting for a cause that had not been approved by the secretary of the public welfare

These Guatemalan refugees were given sanctuary by a church in Germantown, Pennsylvania. They are masked to protect their own identities as well as the lives of relatives in Guatemala.

council. Upon appeal to the state supreme court, Newton and Russell Cantwell's convictions on the breach of the peace charges were reversed, but the remaining convictions were affirmed.

The Supreme Court reversed the convictions. One of the Connecticut laws under which the Cantwells were convicted gave the secretary of the public welfare council the power to deny a certificate of approval to anyone whose cause he or she did not consider to be genuinely religious. According to the Court, "Such a censorship of religion as a means of determining its right to survive is a denial of liberty protected by the First Amendment."

The other law under which Jesse Cantwell was convicted concerned breach of the peace. The Court found that, although the phonograph record Jesse Cantwell played "aroused animosity," the act involved

> no assault or threatening of bodily harm, no truculent bearing, no intentional discourtesy, no personal abuse. On the contrary, we find only an effort to persuade a willing listener to buy a book or to contribute money in the interest of what Cantwell, however misguided others may think him, conceived to be true religion.

The Court made it clear that it is not within a state's power to engage in religious censorship or to forbid individuals from publicly professing their religious beliefs, even if those beliefs are considered offensive or obnoxious by those who do not share them.

Does this man have the right to profess his beliefs even if they offend others?

In 1989, the Minnesota Supreme Court ruled that Amish people cannot be forced to act against their beliefs. This meant they did not have to put a bright orange triangle on their buggies to warn other drivers of a slow-moving vehicle. But in a 1990 Oregon case, the Supreme Court narrowed the constitutional protection of religion when it clashes with the general law. The Minnesota ruling was set aside.

9
Laws Forcing People to Act against Their Beliefs

The Supreme Court has decided, as shown in the previous chapter, that the federal government can prevent or punish certain actions even if those actions are undertaken for sincere religious reasons. Does the same hold true for inaction? Can the government force people to take actions that go against their religious beliefs? Some of the more complex problems concerning free exercise of religion have centered on this question.

Flag Salute

Throughout the early part of the 20th century, many states required students at public schools to salute and pledge allegiance to the flag.

Children who refused to participate in these ceremonies were expelled from school and their parents were subject to criminal prosecution.

These laws posed a problem for Jehovah's Witnesses because they believe that such salutes are forbidden by the Bible. A number of Jehovah's Witnesses decided to accept expulsion rather than break the rules of their religion. A Jehovah's Witness in the Minersville, Pennsylvania, school district, however, took the issue to court.

In 1940, the Supreme Court upheld the Pennsylvania law. The Court declared that: "National unity is the basis of national security... We live by symbols. The flag is the symbol of our national unity, transcending all internal differences, however large, within the framework of the Constitution."

This ruling, unfortunately, provided an excuse for many to act out their hatred against those who disagreed with them. Local school boards used the decision as the basis for adopting new flag salute laws that further harassed Jehovah's Witnesses. For two years after the decision was announced, Jehovah's Witnesses throughout the country were attacked. Angry mobs drove some of them out of their homes and forced them to leave the cities in which they lived. In Maine, a Jehovah's Witness church was burned.

The violence that was touched off by the Court's decision weakened the justices' argument that national unity can be achieved by symbols. In addition, the decision came under heavy criticism from judges, lawyers, educators, and representatives of many faiths. When the Supreme Court received another appeal involving compulsory flag salute in

School children pledge allegiance to the flag. In 1943, the Supreme Court reversed its 1940 decision by declaring that the compulsory flag salute was unconstitutional.

1943, these factors influenced its decision. Of the eight justices who had voted with the majority in 1940, three said that they had been wrong, and two were no longer members of the Court. The 1943 Supreme Court ruling declared compulsory flag salutes unconstitutional.

Justice Robert Jackson, one of the new members of the Court, wrote the majority opinion. He said that the freedoms of speech, press, assembly, and worship may be restricted only to prevent grave and immediate danger to interests of the state. In an oft-quoted passage, Jackson said:

> If there is any fixed star in our Constitutional constellation, it is that no official, high or petty, can prescribe what shall be orthodox in politics, nationalism, religion, or other matters of opinion, or force citizens to confess by words or act their faith therein.

Conscientious Objectors

Even when the founders of the United States were fighting for independence, they recognized the right of **conscientious objection**, the refusal to serve in the armed forces because of religious beliefs, to war. The Continental Congress of 1775 promised to respect the beliefs of those whose religious convictions forbade them to kill fellow human beings under any circumstances.

At various times throughout the history of the United States, there have been laws that require young men to participate in a military draft and to serve in the armed forces if drafted. Even so, exceptions have been granted to those with strong religious objections. Members of the clergy have always been exempt from the draft. When this regulation was challenged in 1917 as an unconstitutional mix of religion and government, the Supreme Court refused to hear the case.

The most difficult problem for draft officials has been trying to determine where to draw the line in excusing people from national duty for religious reasons.

The Selective Service Act limited draft exemptions for conscientious objectors to those whose objections were based on a belief in and relationship to a Supreme Being. Those who objected to war because of political, social, or philosophical views, or a "merely personal moral code" were not excused from military service.

In the 1965 case of *United States v. Seeger*, however, the Court broadened

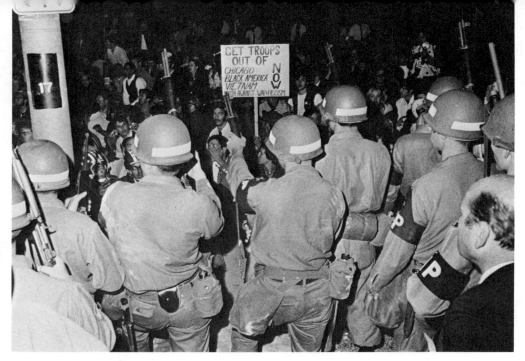

In Chicago, and in cities all over the United States, people protested the U.S. involvement in the Vietnam War.

its definition of conscientious objectors. Those holding a "sincere and meaningful belief" forbidding the use of military arms, even if it was not an orthodox belief in God, could choose an alternate form of service to the country. Five years later, conscientious objection was further expanded to include beliefs based on a personal philosophy or moral code.

In the 1971 case of *Gillette v. United States*, however, the regulation that "selective" conscientious objection did not entitle a person to an exemption was upheld. In other words,

those who objected only to a particular war were not excused from military service, even if their objections were based on religious grounds. Justice Thurgood Marshall wrote in his majority opinion that "the objector to all war—to all killing in war—has a claim that is distinct enough and intense enough to justify special status while the objector to a particular war does not."

Perhaps the most publicized draft exemption case involved world heavyweight boxing champion Muhammad Ali, formerly Cassius Clay.

In 1967, Clay refused induction into the armed forces based on his religious beliefs. But draft officials were advised by the Department of Justice that the Nation of Islam, or the Black Muslim religion, to which Clay belonged, objected to military service for political and racial reasons, not religious ones. Furthermore, the Department of Justice claimed that Clay's beliefs

> do not appear to preclude military service in any form, but rather are limited to military service in the Armed Services of the United States.... However, only a general scruple against participation in war in any form can support an exemption as a conscientious objector.

Clay's exemption was denied. He was convicted of draft evasion by a federal jury, sentenced to five years in prison, and fined $10,000. The case was appealed to the Supreme Court, which issued its decision in 1971. According to the Court, Clay's refusal to serve was in fact based on religious beliefs, and his conviction was overturned.

In the 1980s, the courts upheld a law requiring every 18-year-old male who is a U.S. citizen, even conscientious objectors, to register for the draft. Failure to register, even on religious grounds, has resulted in convictions.

Government-Imposed Burdens

Courts have reacted strongly against efforts by the government to force people to act against their religious convictions. This was clarified in the 1963 case of *Sherbert v. Verner*. The case involved a Seventh-Day Adventist who was fired for refusing to work on Saturday, which her religion designated as the Sabbath. Her request for unemployment compensation was denied by South Carolina. In the state's view, refusal to accept jobs that required work on Saturday, was, in effect, a refusal to accept employment. Unemployment benefits were not given to those who turned down employment.

The Supreme Court ruled that South Carolina could not deny benefits on that basis. The state had forced a person to violate her religious beliefs in order to become eligible for benefits. In the words of Justice William Brennan, "Government imposition of such a choice puts the same kind of burden upon the free exercise of religion as would a fine imposed against appellant for her Saturday worship."

75

One of the followers of Reverend Sun Myung Moon. Moon was convicted of fraud in 1983.

10
Religious Fraud

What is to prevent someone from using the First Amendment's protection of religion as a shield for fraudulent acts? What if someone uses religion as a front to cheat people out of money and the government out of rightful taxes? Does the government have the power to decide which religious organizations are genuine and which are not?

The courts have ruled that in some cases the government must have the power to make that decision, in order to determine religious fraud. The 1944 case of *United States v. Ballard* offered some guidelines for what the government can do. Guy, Edna, and Donald Ballard had sent out letters asking for contributions to the I AM movement. The letters claimed that Guy Ballard

was a divine messenger. They also claimed that the three Ballards had supernatural power to cure the sick, and that they had already cured hundreds of people. Guy Ballard stated that he had shaken hands with and talked to Jesus, and that he would pass these conversations on to the world.

The Ballards were indicted for using the postal service to obtain money by false representation. Eventually the case made its way to the Supreme Court to decide if this indictment violated the Ballards' right of free exercise of religion.

The Court decided that these people could be convicted of religious fraud. However, it also decided that people could not be convicted of fraud if they sincerely believed in the truth of their claims. A jury's only duty was to decide whether or not the accused was sincere. In the words of the Court:

> Men may believe what they cannot prove. They may not be put to the proof of their doctrines or beliefs. Religious experiences which are as real as life to some may be incomprehensible to others. Yet the fact that they may be beyond the ken [understanding] of mortals does not mean they can be made suspect before the law.

In the Ballard case, the Court found the defendants guilty of fraud because they were insincere in their representations.

Because there is no foolproof way to determine if a person is sincere, judgments in these types of cases are often controversial. One of the most famous verdicts involved the Reverend Sun Myung Moon of the Unification church. Reverend Moon claimed that God had sent him as a messenger of a "new, ultimate, final truth." During the 1970s, Moon's organization generated millions of dollars worth of income and controlled millions of dollars worth of real estate. The state of New York decided that the purpose of the Unification church was not genuinely religious. In 1983, it charged Moon with tax fraud and conspiracy and obtained a conviction. Moon claimed that he was being persecuted simply because of his unpopular religious beliefs. But in 1984, the Supreme Court refused to review his case, and Moon was sentenced to 18 months in prison.

The televangelist Jim Bakker, with his wife Tammy, was convicted on 24 counts of fraud and conspiracy in 1989.

11
You Make the Decision

The following case will give you a chance to further understand some of the issues involving the separation of church and state. What decision would you make if you were a judge in this case?

In 1972, a case involving the clash between the religious beliefs of a community of Amish people and the state of Wisconsin came before the Supreme Court.

The Amish religion teaches its members that modern ways should be avoided. Amish communities do not use modern inventions such as automobiles, television sets, radios, and telephones. Amish parents do not want their children to attend public schools where they will come under pressure to adopt different ideas from those stressed by their religion. Amish children are taught in their own schools where they learn farming, homemaking, and religious values in addition to reading, writing, and arithmetic.

The problem in the case of *Wisconsin v. Yoder* centered on the Amish belief that children do not need schooling beyond the eighth grade. The state of Wisconsin places a strong emphasis on the value of education. In order to protect children from what the state saw as possible parental neglect, it required that all children in the state attend school until age 16.

The Amish could not do this without acting against their religious beliefs, and many broke the law.

Wisconsin attempted to enforce the law. Eventually the matter came before the Supreme Court.

If you were on that Court, how would you rule? Did the Wisconsin law violate the Amish people's right of free exercise of religion? Or were the concerns of the state in this case more important?

In this case, the Supreme Court ruled that the law was an unconstitutional infringement on free exercise of religion. The Court concluded that the Amish way was not "merely a matter of personal preference," but a deep religious conviction. Chief Justice Warren Burger wrote that under United States law, there could be "no assumption that today's majority is 'right,' and the Amish and others like them [are] wrong. A way of life that is odd or erratic but interferes with no rights or interests of others is not to be condemned because it is different." Burger said that the government could infringe upon the religious liberty of the Amish only if it could prove that the state had a "compelling interest in such laws

Amish children learn a song in their community school.

and that no less restrictive alternative exists." In this case, the Court ruled that the interests of the state were not important enough to justify infringement upon the religious liberty of the Amish.

Amish children play during school recess.

The United States Supreme Court building in Washington, D.C., where the Court makes decisions that determine where the "wall of separation" stands.

12
Conclusion

The founders of the United States knew from experience and from history the horrors of religious persecution. The Constitution and the Bill of Rights that they designed were intended to keep the United States from falling into such practices. Religion was declared off limits to government so that both could flourish and so that people could be at peace with their consciences. Government was declared off limits to religious groups who might be tempted to wield the power of the state against rival faiths.

In attempting to carry out this vision of religious freedom, courts in the United States have had a monumental task. They have been forced to find workable answers to questions that have no absolute answers. What is religion? Is the primary purpose of a law religious or secular? Can government pass laws that give indirect aid to religion? Must government go out of its way to avoid aiding religion? When does government neutrality toward religion become "callous indifference" to religion? Which is more important, the interest of the state or the religious freedom of the individual? How sincerely religious are some of the people who collect millions of tax-free dollars from the public?

Complex problems such as these have made the wall of separation between church and state difficult to define and difficult to maintain. Supreme Court Justice Felix

83

Frankfurter said that "agreement... that the First Amendment was designed to erect a 'wall of separation between Church and State' does not preclude a clash of views as to what the wall separates."

That clash of views is much in evidence today. The issues involved in freedom of religion are so large and so complex that honest people can and do hold directly opposite views on many of them. In spite of the many difficulties, however, the United States has succeeded in providing religious freedom for its citizens. As a part of this nation's future, you will have to decide whether this freedom has resulted in the kind of society you want. If so, you will have to guard against the erosion of these liberties. If not, you will have to decide how to change it and whether these changes can be made without endangering the liberty so cherished by the founders of the United States.

This cartoon from the 1870s shows Americans' interest in keeping religion separate from the public schools.

For Further Reading

Kleeberg, Irene Cummings. *Separation of Church and State*. New York: Franklin Watts, 1986.

Kohn, Bernice. *The Spirit and the Letter: The Struggle for Rights in America*. New York: Viking Press, 1974.

Lasky, Kathryn. *Pageant*. New York: Macmillan, 1986.

Lawrence, Jerome and Robert E. Lee. *Inherit the Wind*. New York: Random House, 1955.

Lawson, Don. *Landmark Supreme Court Cases*. Hillside, New Jersey: Enslow Publishers, 1987.

Mabie, Margot C.J. *The Constitution: Reflection of a Changing Nation*. New York: Henry Holt, 1987.

Morris, Richard B. *The Constitution*. Minneapolis, Minnesota: Lerner Publications, 1985.

Speare, Elizabeth George. *The Witch of Blackbird Pond*. Boston: Houghton Mifflin, 1958.

Weiss, Ann E. *God and Government*. Boston: Houghton Mifflin, 1982.

Important Words

The terms listed below are defined on the indicated page:

atheist, 37
conscientious objection, 73
creation, theory of, 55
evolution, theory of, 55
exemption, 60
heretical, 13
Inquisition, 13
Nativity, 61
notary public, 60
parochial school, 10
polygyny, 65
public school, 10
Sabbath, 59
sanctuary, 67
secularism, 51

Index

Acknowledgements

The photographs and illustrations in this book are reproduced through the courtesy of: p. 1, George Overlie; pp. 2, 42, 48 (left), 51, 52, 54, 58, 62, 68, 72, 76, 78, Religious News Service; p. 6, Washington Post; pp. 8, 12, 16, 17, 18, 28, 32, 35, 40, 46, 47, 82, 84, Library of Congress; p. 11, David L. Rose; pp. 14, 27, New York Public Library; pp. 20, 36, Dictionary of American Portraits; pp. 22, 27, 34, Independent Picture Service; p. 25, Thomas Gilcrease Institute; p. 31, Metropolitan Museum of Art; p. 38, American Telephone and Telegraph; p. 41, National Geographic Society; pp. 44, 45 (bottom), Minnehaha Academy; p. 45 (top), Control Data; p. 48 (right), Milton J. Blumenfeld; p. 49, Jeny Nieuwenhuis; pp. 56, 57, Collector's Book Store; p. 61, Minnesota Orchestra; p. 63, Minnesota House of Representatives; p. 64, Museum of the American Indian; p. 66 (top), New York Historical Society; p. 66 (bottom), Utah State Historical Society; p. 69, National Archives; p. 70, Iowa Development Committee; p. 74, UPI; pp. 80, 81, Charles S. Rice.